Guard Your Core

17 Life Lessons on Me, Myself & I

Jay Payne

Copyright 2016 by Jay Payne

All rights reserved. In accordance with the U.S. Copyright Act of 1976, the scanning, uploading, and electronic sharing of any part of this book without the permission of the publisher is unlawful piracy and theft of the author's intellectual property. If you would like to use material from this book (other than for review purposes), prior written permission must be obtained by contacting the publisher at info@knowledgepowerinc.com.

Thank you for your support of the author's rights.

ISBN: 978-0-9967162-9-1 (paperback)
ISBN: 978-0-9976622-2-1 (hardback)
ISBN: 978-0-9976622-7-6 (ebook)
Library of Congress Control Number: 2016939189

Edited by: Penny Scott, Laurel J. Davis
Cover Design: Juan Roberts, Creative Lunacy, Inc.

Published by
Knowledge Power Books
Valencia, California 91355
www.knowledgepowerbooks.com

Printed in the United States of America

To my loving wife Tatiana, who was the key motivation and catalyst behind my writing this book.

Contents

Introduction 1

Part One: The Genesis – How It All Began 3

Chapter 1   The Genesis of Me, Myself & I:
                      The Personality Types 5

Chapter 2   The Genesis of Body, Mind & Spirit:
                      The Core Types 9

Part Two: Identifying & Guarding Your Core Type 13

Chapter 3   What is Your Core? 15

Chapter 4   Core Type – Spirit 19

Chapter 5   Core Type – Mind 25

Chapter 6   Core Type – Body 31

Chapter 7   How to Identify Your Core Type 35

Chapter 8   Hybrids 39

Chapter 9   How to Guard Your Core Type 43

Part Three: Identifying & Managing Your Personality Type........51

Chapter 10 Your Personality Type 53

Chapter 11 The "Me" Personality Type 55

Chapter 12 The "Myself" Personality Type 59

Chapter 13 The "I" Personality Type 65

Chapter 14 How to Manage Your Personality Type.........................71

Chapter 15 Multi-Personalities 75

**Part Four: Core & Personality Type Combinations –
             The Launch and Lift-Off 79**

Chapter 16 Core & Personality Type Combinations........................81

Chapter 17 The Launch and Lift-Off 95

Acknowledgements 101

About the Author... 103

Bibliography 105

Introduction

You are embarking on a journey of self-discovery into "Guarding Your Core" and "Managing Your Personality." Everyone is made up of Body, Mind and Spirit (emotions). Although all are important, which one of these core facets is the most vital one in order for you to feel, function, and produce your very best?

The answer to that question describes your *Core Type*. You must guard and protect your core type in order to attain to and maintain a balanced life. Your core type describes **what** you are. By the same token, each of our personalities is made up of three facets: "Me" (Enjoyment) "Myself" (Safety) and "I" (Control). For most of us, one of these facets is clearly more dominant than the other two. The dominant facet is your *Personality Type*. Your personality type is **who** you are. You must manage your personality type so that it does not consume you to the point of your not being able to maintain balance in your interpersonal relationships.

Guarding your core type and managing your personality type together form the foundation for what and who you are. Are you ready for simple yet revelatory concepts that will help you to attain to and maintain a well-balanced life? The book you are about to read provides life lessons designed to do just that.

PART ONE

The Genesis – How It All Began

CHAPTER 1

The Genesis of Me, Myself & I:

The Personality Types

"Me" – teaches you how to enjoy life
"Myself" – teaches you security and stability
"I" – teaches you self-determination and accomplishment

Your *personality type* is the essence of **who** you are!

My journey began right after I left home as a college freshman. I was struggling to find myself after a very strict and tumultuous upbringing. Classmates considered me a nerdy church boy. It became exhausting trying to change into someone who was more socially exciting or popular. During these formative years of self-discovery, it was divinely revealed to me that there are only three people that I need to worry about: *Me, Myself,* and *I*. Over the course of time, I studied my own personality and that of those around me. I came to realize that there were three distinct parts or facets to everyone's personality. Individually, I call these facets "types." I considered the following personality types:

- **Me:** *The pleasure, fun-seeking and/or enjoyment part of our personality.*
- **Myself:** *The part of ourselves that operates the survival instinct; the safety and stability part.*
- **I:** *The drive for personal accomplishment, self-promotion, control of life's direction and destiny.*

Although collectively these three facets reside within everyone's personality, I became aware via people-watching and self-study that one facet is typically more dominant than the other two. I refer to this dominant facet as an individual's "personality type." In fact, your personality type not only drives and dominates how you go about making decisions, it is also the law for your personal rules of engagement when interacting with other people. My college and subsequent early adulthood years provided the practice field for a lot of hits and misses as I developed and substantialized the concepts.

I learned that not only am I a "Myself " personality type, but the characteristics of being a "Myself " govern all of my actions, conversations, even thoughts and ideas. I discovered that I do not have to assist my personality type, for it is always fighting and pushing to show and express itself. Your personality type is naturally set on autopilot, with the goal to control your life. A "Me" is going to always try to have a good time first. A "Myself" is going to always be guarded – better safe than sorry first. And an "I" will seek to gain and maintain control of his or her life's direction without fail. I had to learn how to manage, resist and discipline my personality type in order to tap into and nurture the other two facets. This is important in order to maintain balance regarding relationships amongst family, friends, bosses, co-workers and beyond. Relationships with our significant other can immediately take a positive turn when we (a) learn to identify and manage our own personality type, and (b) identify and nurture our significant other's personality type.

CHAPTER 2

The Genesis of Body, Mind & Spirit:

The Core Types

Minds – give structure to the world
Spirits – make it go 'round
Bodies – set the pace

Your *core* is the essence of **what** you are!

Years after graduating from college, I started experiencing a series of challenging, life-changing events. As it is for many, life was not working in accordance with my expectations. There was a dramatic flux of change occurring; divorce was on the horizon, my career was in transition, all while dealing with the stress of raising three young children. No matter how hard I tried, I just could not achieve life balance. It was during this time that my former pastor, Harold Hoffman, taught on the triune being of mankind and its importance for balance in life. In addition to the soul, human essence is mind, body and spirit.

Mind, Body and Spirit are the three major facets of our essence. Although all three are significant, one is more dominate and directly affects how we function on a daily basis. I further researched, explored and developed these concepts that he taught along with the personality types – Me, Myself and I – over the next decade. Through my many life experiences, observations and practical discussions and/or counseling with individuals and families, I am convinced that identifying and guarding your core is critical in order to attain and, more importantly, maintain a balanced life.

The three core types are defined as follows:

- ❖ ***Body***: *The human physical form; its sensory perception, physical fitness and health.*
- ❖ ***Mind***: *Logical reasoning; the thought-processing center of our being and the mental organization of expression.*
- ❖ ***Spirit***: *The deep seat of our emotions, feelings, and passions; our internal drive – the fire within.*

After years of much trial and error and achieving results from these concepts within my own life (e.g., career success, inner peace, self-fulfillment, happily married), I started to share these life-changing principles with others. I am convinced that these broad-range principles, properly applied, will help you. Not only because of my own personal failure and success experiences, but also based on my practical experience in the following situations:

- ❖ insight and practical counseling
- ❖ public interaction
- ❖ corporate leadership positions
- ❖ cleric and ecclesiastical leadership

My professional career experience has certainly added depth and practicality to this written work. I have reached the executive ranks by building a successful career covering more than 30 years of effectively working in various manufacturing industrial environments within the field of Quality Assurance and Control. I've been fortunate to lead and mentor individuals, teams and companies in problem-solving, data trend analysis, corrective actions, process/system improvements and team-building techniques. My focus has been to be a subtle, effective catalyst for positive change. It has also been to transform mere functional groups into efficient, mission-driven, productive, and caring teams.

This, in parallel with my over twenty-five years of clerical experience and service, has allowed me to transition the use of these principles to both bring about and increase quality assurance within people's lives. This book, **Guard Your Core: 17 Life Lessons on Me, Myself &I,** contains principles that have helped dozens of relationships, marriages, and even managerial and human resources matters regarding employee behavior and development. These concepts have even been applied in order to gain a better understanding of customer service from both the custom-er/client *and* the service agent/employee perspectives. Get ready for the revelatory ride of your life, and I sincerely hope that you enjoy reading this book.

PART TWO

Identifying

&

Guarding Your Core Type

CHAPTER 3

What is Your Core?

The essence of **what** you are

As I mentioned in Part One, all of us are made up of the core facets of Body, Mind and Spirit. These are the vital elements of what makes us functioning human beings. They all must be guarded, protected and nurtured. However, your core type is the one vital element that outweighs the other two in its importance for you to be efficient, effective and at your very best. It is, in essence, what you are.

For instance, I personally am a Body core type. That means that my whole center of balance is predicated on how I feel physically. When I am mentally (Mind) or emotionally (Spirit) overwhelmed, it does not even come close to a negative impact perspective as compared to when I am overwhelmed physically (Body) by stress from illness or exhaustion. When my Body is off, then I am off. For me, it is tougher to focus with a physical issue than with an emotional or mental one. In fact, most people would guess me to be a Mind due to my mission-oriented intensity. However, your core type is not necessarily your area of strength; it typically shows itself more strongly when you are at your weakest. It will speak loudly and proudly when you are under duress. It will also linger around the longest in regards to the time you require for healing or recuperation.

Your personality type can change. We will discuss that in later chapters. However, your core type cannot change. It is your modus operandi and the axis for your life's operation. A Spirit will always be a Spirit; a Mind, a Mind; and a Body, a Body. For clarity's sake, it may be helpful for you to think of your core type as a vehicle type, for example, SUV/truck, sports car or sedan. An SUV will always be an SUV. Even if you try to change it by adding a sports car engine, tuning and tires, it is still in essence an SUV that has been souped-up or tricked-out, so to speak. By the same token, you can alter a sports car to handle rough terrain, but that won't make it an SUV. It is still a sports car, only altered. Similarly, you can add to or alter your core type, but it will still be the same one. Your core type is your core type. Are you getting the picture?

It follows, then, that your core type essentially defines what you are. That is important because it identifies the area that needs even more focus, attention and care than the other core facets if you are to live a balanced life. We will discuss this more in Chapter 9, "How to Guard Your Core Type." But first, within the next few chapters we will break down the different core types.

CHAPTER 4

Core Type:

Spirit

A *Spirit* gives *emotional* connectivity, bonding and hope.

(1) Spirits are fluid like water, elastic, and resist being controlled

What do I mean when I say "Spirit"? A Spirit is a person whose main modus operandi is both governed and driven by their emotions. Their internal feelings and emotions govern their overall sense of well-being and the majority of their decisions and actions. The most frequent reaction will be within their feelings first versus their mind or body. The emotional energy of fiery fight or saddened flight is what arises first. Spirits experience the emotional rise similar to an adrenaline rush (fight) or the deflating of a balloon (flight) in their feelings: fear, anger, sadness and excitement, just to name a few. Spirits are the most plentiful of the three main core types; roughly 50 percent of the entire population are Spirits.

In recent years, perhaps the biggest surprise discovered during my observations and research has been just how many men are Spirits. Society often highlights the emotional nature of women, but the emotional nature of Spirit men is just as great, if not greater! Since Spirits are emotionally fluid, they are the most unpredictable and the most spontaneous of the core types. Therefore, they tend not to operate well in forced situations or circumstances. I call this involuntary containment. Spirits are only happy in situations where they agree to the containing environment. When I say containment, I mean relationship, job, career, school, group, church, etc. When a Spirit is unhappy with their containing environment, believe you me, everyone within their circle of influence will be aware of their unhappiness. Oftentimes, they move through multiple jobs, careers, relationships, schools, etc. Of all the core types, Spirits are the most likely to make a move or change due to their fluid and sometimes restless nature.

The goal is not so much for Spirits to stop making changes but rather to take more time to reason through their options thoughtfully and weigh all of the pros and cons prior to deciding whether to make the move or stay. Freedom of movement, change and spontaneity is a priority for Spirits and a natural part of their inner wiring, so to speak. Impulse can be both a friend and an enemy to a Spirit. Spirits need their emotional gas tanks constantly refilled or re-energized. Both the amount and the frequency of the replenishing or re-energizing are unique to the individual. However, when the emotional energy is low, the Spirit will be down as well.

Problems often arise when Spirits hold others accountable for refilling their emotional gas tank rather than holding themselves responsible for guarding and replenishing it. They must not only be aware of when their emotional energy is falling below the low fuel level mark but also develop precautions to conserve and refill as needed.

Spirits tend to judge life based on human interactions. Very few Spirits can tolerate being alone frequently or for long periods of time, "Myself" personality types often being the exception. Spirits are naturally prone to networking. If you have ever heard of the term "know no strangers," you can be sure that speaks of a Spirit. Most of them judge their happiness in life based on successful human interaction and networking.

(2) Spirits are the glue that holds humanity together.

Spirits are atmosphere changers. They can affect the mood of a group, a conversation, or an environment, such as at work, like no one else. They cannot be ignored. Feelings and emotions often do not make sense and they cannot always be explained, but they are there. With a Spirit, it is not about making sense per se, but rather a recognition, acknowledgement and acceptance of the importance of both their and other people's feelings. For Spirits, feelings and emotions are seeking to exhibit themselves whether consciously or subconsciously. Since they are fluid, just as if a drink spills out onto the table, attention is grabbed to deal with the spill, either momentarily or longer depending on the impact of the spill.

Spirits demand attention. If it were not for them, we would lose intimacy not only with our own emotions but within our relationships with other people. Spirits require us to recognize feelings, even when those feelings do not make sense. For example, "I'm crying and I don't know why" is a common occurrence. Spirits force the world to at least recognize and accept the importance of emotions and feelings. They cause us to connect in some way. The Mind or Body core may say, "You're not making any sense," but the Spirit says, "That's not an excuse to ignore my feelings." Spirits work to ensure that we do not ignore, forget about or run over each other as we go through life pursuing our goals.

(3) Spirits react strongly within the conflict spectrum: fight or flight.

Spirits tend to fall into one of two categories: fight or flight. What I mean by this is that their emotional energy and feelings will either be prone to emotional defensiveness and be very sensitive to being challenged or attacked, or they will be withdrawn, shut down and maybe even disappear when under duress. In rare cases, some Spirits are more middle of the road between the two spectrums. No matter where they reside within the spectrum, they all have the ability to go from one end to the other fairly quickly if the need arises. This makes Spirits the most unpredictable of the three core types and is a major reason why they cannot be ignored. It is also why I call them the glue that holds humanity together and helps to keep us connected.

Another characteristic of Spirits is that of magnetic polarization. In the same way that magnets come together or their poles repel, that is exactly how Spirits interact and connect with people. Nothing is more intriguing than witnessing two Spirits meet for the first time and connect and even bond as they interact, as if they have been friends for many years. We all have the ability to do that, but only a Spirit has the actual propensity for it. By the same token, Spirits can size each other up and just like magnets with like poles, they can repel each other and be simply unable to connect. Trying to get opposing Spirits to connect is like mixing oil and water – it won't happen.

The goal of Spirits is to form relationships that connect, with the end goal of bonding in all of their critical connections. An example of the power of a Spirit bonding is found in the biblical story of King David's relationship with Jonathan. David loved Jonathan more than a woman.

This is not referring to a physical or even a mental connection, but rather a spiritual (emotions/feelings) bond. Jonathan loved David so much that his kingly lineage didn't mean anything. Their spirits connected and they had a strong friendship. The bonding of Spirits is so rare that most of us have not connected to anyone in this way and if we have, that person is more than likely our parent, grandparent or in rare cases a dear friend. The best relationships are not based on mental or physical connections. Rather, when Spirits connect, it is the strongest bond possible between two people. Warning: this is not referring to feelings of romantic or sexual attraction. The forming of an emotional bond is much deeper than just feelings, which can change often.

Spirit is inner fire, desire, feelings and belief motivation. It is like fuel that has to be replenished, or a mechanism that occasionally needs a tune-up or service. When a Spirit is low or damaged within their emotions, it is the same as when the physical body needs rest or is ill. A Spirit must be emotionally replenished or strengthened.

Sometimes we don't have a sensible, strategic or logical means to win. However, the right Spirit can walk into the room and get everyone to believe. Almost anytime you hear of the underdog group miraculously defeating the greater opponent, you can be sure that a Spirit is involved somewhere. They make us believe that we can defeat the greater opponent and take the hill! Spirits first *feel* that they can, then they *think* that they can. That's why history is full of military figures, coaches and even religious leaders who were Spirits. Spirits rarely say that it doesn't matter how they feel because most of the time how they feel is absolutely important to them. When strategy is gone due to overwhelming obstacles or losses, there must be something to keep the troops or teams together, and it better be a Spirit who has an emotional bond with the group to encourage them to believe and hope against no hope. There is a difference between the spirit of unity (mental) and unity of the spirit (emotional bond). When Spirits unite to believe, that's how they overcome. The spirit of unity is short term, but unity of the spirit is long term. This is why emotional gatherings and uprisings often dissipate as quickly as they flared up.

Sometimes Spirits feel they're in control, when they're not. They can feel like they're on top of the world, when they're really not. If they're feeling it, they're on top of the world. Society is more tolerant towards imbalanced Spirits. Society develops accommodations for mental and physical imbalances, but not so much for emotional imbalances. Most imbalanced Spirits just go about their normal daily lives.

I have always used Cameron Diaz as the poster child for a balanced Spirit. Other examples of Spirits include: Donald Trump, Joe Biden, Nancy Grey, Robin Williams, Whitney Houston, Mariah Carey, Kanye West and Kevin Hart.

Terms of Endearment for Spirits:
- Spirits give us hope.
- Spirits help us to believe that we can win against all odds, even when it doesn't make sense.
- The life of the party will in all likelihood be a Spirit.
- Spirits are the most prone to expressing their feelings.
- Spirits created the expression, "You are only as young as you feel." They also created statements such as "50 is the new 40," "We connected and bonded as if we knew each other our whole lives," and "It's not over 'til it's over."
- They often know no strangers or at least desire to connect with others.
- They often wear their feelings on their sleeves.
- Networking is a natural ability.
- Spirits hate the feeling of being alone.

CHAPTER 5

Core Type:

Mind

Minds have *logical* sensibility

(1) Being a Mind has nothing to do with smartness or intelligence.

Without a doubt, the biggest risk and danger associated with this book is the fact that most people automatically believe that a Mind is the best core type to be because we associate it with being successful. Consequently, most people really try to prove or convince themselves that they are Minds. This is a big mistake, because misdiagnosing your core can be devastating. Remember the vehicle type analogy. What value is there to not accepting that your SUV is an SUV and not a sports car? You can damage your core by misusing it, ignoring warning signs, and not performing maintenance checks just as it would your vehicle.

Being a Mind does not speak to intelligence. Spirits and Bodies do just as well on I.Q. tests, in higher education and in career success. Being a Mind means that you regularly operate in logical reasoning with limited or no emotion. Things must make logical sense to a Mind. Emotions and feelings are often perceived as weaknesses. Because of this, Minds tend to be able to focus on the task at hand quickly and stay on target – that is, until they are either bored or mentally exhausted.

Minds can easily and regularly block out their emotions and feelings, often categorizing them as distractions. They most certainly can get emotional, but only as it is tied to a principle they strongly believe in or after they have well thought out the ramifications. They can become so mission or task-driven to the point of being dismissive of others' feelings; it's just their nature.

Minds gave birth to the "mind over matter" and "I think I can, therefore I can" concepts. However, when a Mind's plan falls apart, they are distraught and often cannot bounce back as quickly as a Spirit after a plan fails due to the fact that they operate on detailed thought and principle. Since they pride themselves on regularly figuring things out, results of failure are often difficult for Minds to deal with, especially regarding situations that they hold dear. Minds weigh the worth of the current circumstance in light of its ability to positively impact the future direction where they are headed. To constantly weigh the pros and cons (the worth) is important to a Mind. By comparison, a Spirit weighs their feelings on a matter equally with the pros and cons.

I find it interesting to observe women who are "Minds" in the dating world. Spirit women outnumber Mind women almost three to one. Therefore, most dating tactics of men have been built and formulized to focus on a strategy that emphasizes making a positive impact on women's emotions and feelings initially. When a man dates a Mind for the first time, it can often be awkward, uncomfortable and even downright embarrassing for him. Minds focus more on direction – "Why is this occurring and where is this headed?" – rather than emotionally weighing the impact of the moment. The meeting of the minds is more important than a sweet gesture. Mentally intriguing and stimulating conversation cannot be understated for a Mind, male or female.

Another characteristic of a Mind is that when they truly make a decision after their mind is made up, it will often take a miracle or an act of Congress to change it. Lack of patience is sometimes an issue for Minds. Minds pride themselves on the ability to make firm decisions and usually require limited to no input from the outside. This is not always a good approach, mainly because a Mind may miss the human emotional impact regarding their decision. When counseling couples, I have learned that there is a big difference when a Spirit says that they don't care versus when a Mind says it. Spirits speak from the emotions or feelings and therefore we must ascertain the depth and cause of those feelings. However, a Mind has drawn a definite conclusion and more often than not, when they say "they don't care," they are really at that point. A made-up mind of a Mind core type is a force to be reckoned with.

In "Star Trek," my all-time favorite TV show, Spock strives to keep himself disconnected from his emotions. He has little need for friendship because when we're out of touch with our emotions, we lose connectivity with people. It may work on TV but not in real life.

Of the three core types, Minds are the strongest from a resistance to damage perspective, but at the same time they are the ones with the most to lose. This is because the Mind is the most difficult of the core types to heal from damage. Think with me on this. Spirits can be heartbroken and heal. It may not be easy and some recover better than others. However, for the most part, they are able to revive and recover eventually like no one else because of the fluidity and elasticity of feelings and emotions. As for a Body, they can get sick or break bones and for the most part throughout life they are able to heal. Even when a Spirit or a Body core type does not heal fully, they can still usually function. However, what is a broken or damaged Mind? A mental breakdown for a Mind is cataclysmic. Even if there is recovery, they are never the same. One day, I would like to conduct a survey study amongst Alzheimer's patients. I believe there is a connection, not of the disease diagnosis to the Mind core type per se, but rather to the rate of their deterioration. I believe speed of decline may be tied to the Mind core. For when your core deteriorates rapidly, then you will also. For Spirits with similar chronic illnesses, when the will to live and the emotional fight is gone, then that person will deteriorate rapidly. I've observed mental illness. Oftentimes Spirits will not even acknowledge their mental condition. Their spirit can fill the void even to the point that they can feel they're the ones who are normal and everyone else is different.

Never under estimate the power and fortitude of a Spirit to hope and believe even when it doesn't logically make sense. My father is a Spirit, a fiery fighting one at that. Even though he has had multiple strokes, cannot walk without assistance and is 77 years old, he still is going to start a church, a business, a book and numerous other ventures. Even though his mind and body are deteriorating, his Spirit core remains strong. Remember, when your core is strong, you will feel strong even when the other two facets are on the decline. But if your core is weak, you will be weak even if the other two facets are strong. Your core carries the majority vote always, so guard your core!

The power of being a Mind is noteworthy, too, however. I have met more than one former drug addict who describes their recovery as just one day they decided to stop using drugs. Several said there was little struggle at all when their mind was made up.

(2) Minds meet purposefully: iron sharpens iron.

There are some Minds who have nothing in common with the lifestyles of fellow Minds, but they have a strong mental connection. With a Spirit, it's more about emotional bonding; but with a Mind, it's about a mental connection. Minds can have a friend they haven't seen for a great period of time, and the only time they meet may be for business, yearly gatherings or the like in order to reconnect and exchange. The meeting of the Minds, as it were, is like an electrical charge. The exchange of thoughts and ideas on the same wavelength is very stimulating for a Mind.

Minds tend to handle breakups and departures differently. It may be difficult to acknowledge that the breakup, separation or departure is necessary, but once a Mind comes to the conclusion that it is necessary, they can seemingly disconnect with an almost heartless, absolute resolve. Minds are able to say, "We just didn't connect anymore."

In most relationships, where we're going is important, but for a Mind, it is almost everything! You might hear a Spirit say, "We've really bonded and we do our own thing." However, for a Mind, emotional bonding is secondary. "Where are we headed?" and "Where are we going?" are almost an automatic program for Minds, even in relationships.

Minds can at times struggle with being patient with people. Spirits are aware that bonding takes time and they are usually surprised when it happens quickly. However, Minds just plug in and look for a charge.

When they don't connect the first time, they're not inclined to connect the second time on an interpersonal level. When a Mind or a Spirit asks a question, a Spirit is more interested in *how* the question is being answered, whereas a Mind is more focused on *what* the answer is. Minds struggle with insomnia more than the other core types. It is often difficult for a Mind to shut down.

(3) Mind's judge

Minds just want things to make sense and they can be dismissive when things do not. They are constantly judging, sizing up and drawing conclusions on matters, people and circumstances. To this end, they can come across as being cold or insensitive, especially when in positions of power and authority. "My way or the highway or no way," was a Mind initiated statement. Minds can often lack empathy, and they sometimes struggle with compassion.

Examples of Minds include: Tom Cruise, Ted Kopple, Kobe Bryant, Oprah Winfrey, Denzel Washington, Peyton Manning, Hillary Clinton, President Obama and Scarlett Johansson.

Terms of Endearment for Minds:
- Mind over matter.
- My way or the highway.
- That doesn't make any sense.
- Let's think this through.
- I think I can.
- Think rationally or logically.
- Some things are just more important than feelings.
- That's dumb or stupid.
- An idle mind is the devil's workshop.
- My mind is playing tricks on me.

CHAPTER 6

Core Type:

Body

Bodies say, "Let's just go, *get moving* and get it done."

Of the three core types, the Body is the most difficult to identify. The main reason for this is that as humans we are all aware and sensitive to the physical feelings and messages within our physical bodies. For instance, when we have a cold or some other illness, or even if we are just tired, we exhibit similar reactions and expressions. We react and verbalize them similarly. However, for the Body core type, those physical feelings and messages speak more powerfully and clearly than the mind's thought processes or the feelings of emotion.

Another reason for the difficulty in identifying the Body type is because misidentification can spurn from a chronic medical condition, such as migraines or stomach illnesses. A person who is constantly affected by physical challenges or medical conditions is not necessarily a Body core type.

Sometimes people are misidentified as Bodies because we tend to assume that health nuts or the extremely lazy would be in this group. But nothing could be further from the truth. For the record, as previously mentioned, the author of this book is unequivocally a Body.

(1) A Body is driven by their physical well being.

One of the surprises during my years of research is that the other core types are often surprised or even bewildered when a Body sometimes cannot explain in detail what the physical problem is when there is an issue. Most people are able to adequately describe how they feel physically and often with great detail. It's not so much that a Body can't describe it or explain it, but a Body is more aware of and sensitive to the chain reactions within their bodies that are impacted by a specific problem and therefore often cannot separate the totality of the issues. For instance, for a Body, a fever is never just a fever but it impacts and equally affects something else negatively. A headache is not just a headache but merely an outcry of pain ignited by discomfort messages from somewhere else within the body.

Just as for Minds and Spirits when they feel overwhelmed, anxious or depressed and cannot adequately describe why at times, so it is physically for a Body. For a Spirit, when their emotions are feeling low, they often cannot describe in detail why they feel depressed inside. So it is with a Body and their interpretations of what is going on inside them physically at times. One thing is for sure, however. A Body is impacted in ways the other two core types are not when physical and/or health issues arise.

Bodies have a tough route for wellbeing as well. Both a Spirit and a Mind can grow stronger and sharper with age. Spirits can actually gain more spirit energy in their senior years than in their younger years on occasion. Minds can become sharper especially once they learn how to guard and nurture their core. Science has yet to find a way to measure spirit. Spirit volume is immeasurable; it depletes yet replenishes. By the same token, science is still baffled regarding the brain's seemingly unlimited capacity. However, when it comes to the limits of the human body as it ages, well, no matter how many plastic surgeries, pills, fluids, etc., the age process still befalls us all, and it bites with intensity on a Body Core type. This of course does not mean that Body types cannot live long and productive lives.

However, we all know that as the body ages, it deteriorates. Therefore, with a Body, the importance of guarding your core becomes even more critical. We can probably recall friends or acquaintances who were loose and reckless Spirits or Minds who wasted their youth and abused their bodies but recovered just fine. For a Body core type, however, the recovery rate drops drastically. A Body cannot reverse the time wasted from long-term physical damage caused by reckless living. The sooner a teenager or young adult learns they are a Body, the better off they are and the sooner they can actually start making lifestyle changes that will take care of their physical health for long-term balance and wellbeing.

A Body definitely would not be the first one to say, "50 is the new 40" or "You're only as young as you feel." In the sports world, when you keep hearing of athletes returning to the game after retirement, more than likely, they're not a Body core type.

Again, let me re-emphasize that being a Body has nothing to do with being prone to pursuing physical fitness or health. Actually, all core types need to focus on self-improvement in those areas. For the Body core type, however, the importance of rest and knowing what foods to avoid will help prevent harm to their unique individual physiology. Body core types have a high sensitivity to physical energy use, stamina and the ability to know if a task can be accomplished or is even worth accomplishing when weighed against impact or cost to their body. I've also observed that many people can still talk normally or even become more chatty when they are ill, but there will be a noticeable reduction in verbal communication when a Body is ill. When a Body is ill or tired, even the tongue is impacted and talking is reduced.

The last point I want to mention is that the greatest challenge with being a Body is that it is the only core type forced to deal with aging head on, since it is our bodies that age and deteriorate more naturally and swiftly than our spirits or minds over time. This core also has a heightened sense of touch.

Terms of Endearment for Bodies:
- A Body usually will not buy into "50 is the new 40," type of statements.
- Bodies invented the power nap.
- A Body will over-emphasize illness; the world stops when a Body is in physical pain: "When I'm sick, I feel like I am dying."
- "That is a waste of energy."
- A Body will not allow their sincere physical effort to be belittled as nothing by someone else.
- "Don't work yourself to death."

CHAPTER 7

How to Identify Your Core Type

Core type - global populace breakdown from observation:
Spirit =50% of the population
Mind =30% of the population
Body =15% of the population

(The last five percent is being left out on purpose and will be discussed in the next chapter.)

Many of you by this point have already identified your core type. Some of you have not yet or are still unsure. Either way, the following points provide the roadmap and insight for identifying your core. Nailing it down can prove to be difficult, but it is critical that you identify your core type to achieve and maintain life balance.

(1) Your core type is the one that reacts the most often and fastest when under duress. Notice that I did not say it reacts the strongest. There is a point and time where all of the different core facets within us will react strongly at different times. There are tragic situations in life that could cause any or all of them to react strongly. Mental, emotional and physical breakdowns do occur and no one is completely exempt from them. Your first impulse reaction that has the highest frequency of occurrence is a good starting point in identifying your core type.

For example, Spirits feel the emotional disturbance and its rise within first. Whether that's the impulse to "fight or flight," you will know if you're a Spirit by your initial reaction. Often this reaction is an almost uncontrollable urge to speak out verbally or lash out in some physical manner. By that I mean it can range from crying or shutting down, to arguments or even physical altercation.

Minds experience an overwhelming mental overload or confusion. Before the emotion takes over, a Mind will run a natural gambit of questions within first. How did this happen? Why did this happen? And most importantly, how do I fix it or make it better? The answer to those questions can certainly spark emotions, but a Mind will not go the emotional route without certain key questions being answered. Body core types may experience upset stomach, cold sweats, rashes, muscle spasms or some other physical reaction.

(2) Your core type's reaction will linger the longest after a stressful situation has ended. Even when the incident that has caused you stress is over, you're often left still grappling with the aftermath within your core type. Spirits will work to come to grips with or reconcile their feelings, a Mind will work to make sense of what occurred and develop a rectification plan, and a Body will deal with whatever physical signs exhibited.

(3) You are at your best when you feel re-energized and motivated within your core type first. For example, a Spirit is at their best when they feel strong and happy within their emotions. It does not matter if the details still have to be mentally thought out. The desire and feeling that it can be done comes from the Spirit core. Mental motivation and stimulation is completely different. When a Mind is energized, they strategically think and see a plan's workable outcome; that's their motivation, namely, the ability to see the details that will bring about the expected outcome. For a Body, even if the emotions and mental faculties are energized, only when they feel physically strong with no discomfort or pain are they feeling their best regarding energy and motivation.

(4) Ask your spouse or significant other (after they read the definitions, of course) for their opinion of what your core type is.

(5) Then, ask your best friend, sibling, parent and/or a close co-worker for their opinion of what you are, just to gain more insight and perspective.

(6) Lastly, know that sometimes identifying your core type can be difficult simply because you have instinctively and through experience learned how to guard it. Some people have achieved balance to the point that their core type does not readily stand out above the other core facets. I have met Spirits who have learned to guard their emotions so well that I could not readily tell that they were Spirits until after I had spent more time with them and got to know them. In these cases, it may take longer, but the roadmap insight outlined above will still work.

CHAPTER 8

Hybrids

You may be a *Hybrid*, but more than likely you are a *Spirit*.

If the biggest risk is to avoid identifying yourself as a Mind when you're not one, then the second biggest risk is not to automatically jump to the conclusion that you are none of the three core types. However, a very small portion of the populace falls into a fourth core type category. I call this the "Hybrid" group.

Most people I meet are either Spirits or Minds. A small percentage are Bodies, and an even smaller percentage are what I call "Hybrids." This core type consists of those who seem to have no clear core type that stands out, or two of the three seem to be almost equal to each other and the person seems to vacillate between them. Hybrids consist of those who have approximately 60 percent of one core facet and 40 percent of another. They are unique in that they are a blend of two core facets.

One important thing to note is that one of the cores of a Hybrid will always be Spirit. Recall the glue and bonding nature of a Spirit? This allows for it sometimes to almost blend itself to another core facet. Again, Hybrids are extremely rare and are less than 5 percent of the populace. Most of us have enough trouble trying to guard one core type. Those who find themselves having to guard more than one can probably now grasp the reality of why keeping life balance is often so difficult.

Another aspect of Hybrids is that their Spirit and other core facet seem to react almost equally under duress. For instance, I know a Hybrid who will immediately start reasoning and planning when trouble comes but almost without fail also show equal emotion. They are a Spirit/Mind. In another example, I know of someone who I thought was a Spirit but when they are physically ill, they are more negative than any Body core type I have ever met and they refuse to even try to function. She is a Spirit/Body. Over the years I have talked to dozens upon dozens, even hundreds of people. I cannot think of more than three Hybrids whom I have personally met. Most suspect Hybrids would be better off accepting that they are Spirits if their Spirit overrides the other core facet 60 percent or more of the time. However, if this is not true, then you may indeed be a Hybrid.

Once a Hybrid core is identified, I recommend that the person not waste time over-analyzing their core type blend percentages. I will say that in almost all cases for Hybrids, the Spirit rules. For this reason, I have often had to break the news to those who self-identify as a Hybrid that they really are a Spirit. I have seen limited cases where the other core facet (either Mind or Body) acts as a gate holding back the emotion that equally arises in challenging situations, but still that emotion seeps through the gate. The important thing for Hybrids to realize is that they essentially have two core types that they must guard in order to maintain a balanced life. Therefore, Hybrids have an arduous task to guard dual cores and it is not a challenge to be taken lightly. In the automobile world, having a Hybrid may be a badge of public honor, but within the core type world it is not. That is not to say that it is a negative; it is just that the work required to guard Hybrid cores cannot be overstated.

CHAPTER 9

How To Guard Your Core Type

Identifying and guarding your core type is the most important point of this book. If we use the vehicle analogy again, not understanding your core is like a driver not knowing what type of vehicle they're driving and, more importantly, not knowing the damage that can be caused by operating the vehicle in a manner it was not designed for.

For instance, a sports car cannot be driven on rugged, off-road terrain regularly without eventually breaking down or malfunctioning. It is a sports car and, as such, it is designed for speed and racetrack-like conditions. Now, that's not to say that a sports car cannot be driven off-road. In order to be successful, however, certain precautions must be taken with the car's mechanical systems. Safety measures must also be followed regarding the way it is driven over the rugged terrain in order for it to operate effectively and to avoid damage. When a person is unaware of their core type, they are in danger of maltreatment or abusing themselves. My intent is certainly not to say that people are just like cars, but rather to illustrate the point that guarding your core type is simply identifying, protecting and nurturing it in order for you to effectively and more successfully operate in pursuit of your life goals. This is what is meant by life balance.

The first steps in guarding your core type are to:

(1) Understand the "Danger Zones." A person should know what attacks or weakens their core, especially the detrimental actions and behaviors that are self-inflicted. I will use myself as an example. Being a Body core type, I learned during my college years that although my friends could eat cold pizza at midnight and still get up feeling okay for a 7 a.m. class, I could not. I learned that if I ate certain foods at night, it would negatively impact my body and I would not be raring to go the next day. Now, a person may say that could be true for anyone, but my point is that, since my core type is Body, eating late had a greater detrimental impact for me.

Remember, your core type is the voice of power among your core facets from a life balance standpoint. Fatigue is a danger zone for all of the core types. Spirits need to avoid or prepare in advance for situations that they know may ignite or provoke anger or sadness. For Minds, it is identifying and preparing for situations that will cause mental overload at work, home, etc. Attempting to "save the world," especially family, is a common danger zone for Minds. Lastly, for Bodies, it is protection from illness, such as dressing appropriately for inclement weather, avoiding disagreeable foods, physical exertion, etc.

(2) Have an escape route. Just as we are taught what to do in case of fire, create escape routes or have a pressure relief valve in case of emergencies affecting your core. Learn how to defuse tension and stresses that attack your core. For a Spirit, it may be learning how to sense escalating conversations and defuse them or excuse yourself and walk away. Spirits should also avoid making important decisions when they are emotional. Making impulsive moves or rash decisions regarding quality of life are often regrettable. It is perplexing the number of Spirits who accept being magnets for drama, simply because they feel they have to. Think of long-term ramifications. Many out of control wildfires began with a small unassuming flame and before you know it, it's grown out of control. For a Mind, it may be learning how to take breaks throughout the day or how to let things go that mentally demand your attention and cause you to lose focus on more important matters. Everyone should incorporate recharging and recuperation time within their daily, weekly and monthly schedules.

(3) Develop all of your core facets with special emphasis on improving the health of your specific core type. Diet, exercise and personal development (education, training and being mentored) help to promote the health and balance of body, mind and spirit. In addition, Spirits must learn how to calm themselves and foster inner peace and should take responsibility for themselves in order to avoid causing a needy, leeching type of effect. A Mind needs to be stimulated with mental pursuits ouside of their required responsibilities; examples can range from puzzles and on-line games, to seminars and classes. A Body should focus on eating habits, sleeping patterns and body movement. I say body movement instead of exercise because keeping the body moving on purpose is the goal. Muscle atrophy is the enemy for a Body. Even in advanced age, a Body core type must keep moving.

(4) Deal with the vain imaginations. Specifically, Spirits are the consummate dreamers, which certainly is a positive. Being wired to see the glass as half full is beneficial. However, Spirits should be on guard against living their feelings of fantasy, thinking what could have been or what they hope to be is reality when it is not. Living the dream is relative. Over-assuming is a constant temptation for a Spirit.

In contrast, Minds are the consummate realists and, as such, can be extremely judgmental and closed-minded. Minds should be on guard against living a mental creation of a world that they perceive as real but no one else does, as if it's your world and you're the only one living in it. Instead, they need to learn how to feel the world and not just seek to know it. Also, having a realistic perception of the world as it is today should be based in part on feedback from others as well.

Bodies should be on guard to avoid exaggerating negative circumstances based on how they are feeling physically. The urge to curl up, shut people out and die, or at least until the crisis passes, should be resisted.

In summary, the practical ways of *guarding your core* areas are as follows:

Mind

1) It is imperative to learn how to rest your mind. A unique characteristic of a Mind is that the mind and body are often not tired simultaneously and therefore do not rest simultaneously. Insomnia is more prevalent among Minds and is often caused by a tired body but a hyperactive mind.

Developing rest patterns for your mind is important. This often requires unwinding prior to bed. Mental distractions that bring peace and relaxation should be pursued.

2) Learn how to stimulate your mind by finding mental activities that disengage you from your normal daily activities. I like to say, "Learn how to unplug from the matrix." Games, puzzles, reading and hobbies that require concentration and focus are all examples of mental distractions that often bring about relaxation for the Mind. It is similar to the affect that the power nap has for the Body core type, or that soothing music or meditation has for the Spirit core type.

3) Remember, imagination is a force of the Mind and must be controlled. The mind plays tricks on all of us; but when a Mind core type allows the mind to play those tricks, it can become a real event with life-altering impact. Have you ever wondered about those stories of individuals who were able to live two different lives for a long period time without other people even suspecting anything? Living dual lives is often associated with imbalanced Minds. Sometimes, imbalanced Minds can't distinguish their own vivid imagination about themselves from reality. This is not a knock on Minds but rather an alert regarding how powerful the mind can be.

Tiger Woods is a Mind. Not even he knew how important family and his mental control ability was to his core type before his infamous incident. His game was forever changed due to his damaged core. He did have some physical ailments before the infamous incident, but they did not impact his game and he was still winning. At that time his Mind core was solid and strong and overcame issues with his other core facets, Body and Spirit. However, it was only after that unfortunate incident that the physical ailments not only increased but are increasingly becoming insurmountable. The mental edge of his core was negatively impacted first.

Kobe Bryant is a Mind. I'm sure it was a difficult journey for him to mentally reconcile his mental belief of himself being the NBA's best player with the reality that Father Time waits for no one. At some point his imagination had to accept the reality that his body had aged and that the career-threatening injuries were continuing to mount. Dressing age-appropriately is another example of the struggle to let it go, if you read between the lines of what I mean. Think: the senior citizen walking on the beach in a Speedo or thong swim trunks.

4) It is important that Minds do not look at emotions as a weakness, especially when developing interpersonal relationships.

5) Minds need to accept that they do not have to understand everything and that everything doesn't have to make sense. When dealing with people, there is an element of unpredictability. To dismiss this fact is a critical error.

6) Due to the unpredictability of feelings, pre-judging and quickly sizing up people is often not a correct approach when dealing with others. Use your judging skills judiciously. Admitting when you are wrong or changing your mind as a result of feelings, are not signs of weakness.

7) Patience is a virtue; be patient with people.

8) Remember, you are "Mind over matter." If you focus and strategize mentally, then you can overcome and achieve.

Spirit

1) Do not get caught up asking, "Why am I this way?" Instead, "Why am I feeling this way?" is the better question. Being emotional is not a negative. It is better to accept the reality and develop counter-measures to control your feelings and to develop release mechanisms for negative emotions.

2) Spirits should learn to not overreact. One should fully digest what is being said within reason rather than impulsively respond emotionally. Guard your emotional buttons instead of wearing your emotions on your sleeve.

3) Utilize one or more of the three defense tactics: a) *avoid* obstacles, issues or people before problems can arise; b) *defuse* by changing the

subject, calming down and lowering your voice, or by deferring to a future time or to someone else; or c) *escape* by leaving or walking away from the environment. Spirits who master these tactics tend to stay wellbalanced.

4) Know if you are "fight or flight" (see Chapter Four: Core Type - Spirit). In this way, you can more easily identify the rise of the fire or deflation of the Spirit. Thus, develop strategies to decompress (get calm and relax) or inflate (recharge and motivate) your spirit.

5) As a Spirit, you will always be drawn to connecting and disconnecting with people, similar to magnetic energy and its constant attract-and-repel effect. Trust your Spirit instincts, but do not overreact.

6) Being free-spirited is good only up to a point. Spirits must be contained. Uncontained Spirits barely reach stability, and almost never maintain it. All Spirits who are happy in their relationships, careers and circle of influences had to learn how to not only contain their spirit but also how to be voluntarily accepting and to compromise. If not, the term "living the dream" often is followed by the unpleasant need to "face reality" or "face the music."

7) In order to avoid the pattern of extreme highs and lows that impact not only you but those that love you, developing structure and consistency is required. Commit with your mind and not only with your feelings.

8) Remember, Spirit is fluid and elastic. You can and will bounce back! You help humanity to stay connected emotionally and not just mentally.

Body

1) Realize that you must take care of your body and focus on its wellbeing to maintain balance.

2) Never underestimate the importance and power of sleep and rest. Power naps are recommended.

3) Learn your eating habits and patterns. Eating the wrong thing can impact a Body the same as a Spirit hearing bad news or a Mind feeling overloaded.

4) Physical movement and plenty of it should be your goal. Physical activity is critical for life balance for the Body. I am referring to activities beyond working out. A Body needs more than that, such as nature walks, dancing, sports play, etc. In other words, a Body needs regular doses of stimulating physical activity that they enjoy. The more a Body is only doing what they feel they physically have to do, the more imbalanced they will become.

5) Physical addictions, such as drugs and alcohol, are exponentially more harmful to you than the other core types. Take care of your body.

6) Try a deep tissue massage at regular intervals.

7) Bodies make it happen because, in the end, all great accomplishments require movement and physicality to get things done.

In summary, we have now covered how to identify and guard your core type. This will help you to obtain and maintain a balanced life as you pursue your goals in life (job stability, career and finances). The second half of this book is equally important but in a different way. It contains important information on how to gain and manage healthy interpersonal relationships. Is this possible, you may ask? Yes, once you learn how to identify and manage your personality type and identify and understand the personality type of other people.

PART THREE

Identifying & Managing Your Personality Type

CHAPTER 10

Your Personality Type

The essence of **who** you are.

During our exploratory journey on core type, we used the automobile analogy in order to help bring clarity. Your core type is the kind of vehicle that you are and it cannot be changed, only adjusted. Things are very different when it comes to your personality type, however. Think of your personality type as the kind of driver that you are in your vehicle. You can certainly change the type of driver you are, and that requires more than adjustments. You cannot become a better driver without study, practice and discipline. Identifying, learning and controlling your personality type is critical in achieving life balance, especially in interpersonal relationships.

When you are driving on the freeway, your vehicle type has some relevance to your interaction with other drivers. It is clear, though, that how you drive, or the type of driver you are, is much more critical to how you relate to other drivers. Similarly, your personality type drives and dictates your relationship with others. Part Three of this book will help you to better understand others. Far too often, we size each other up and then draw wrong conclusions or make erroneous judgments about one another. We often do this based on selfish or, at best, clueless opinion without any sound basis for understanding why a person may act or react in a particular manner.

It is a fact that interpersonal difficulties will occur across all relationships in life – e.g., friendships, marriages, family, co-workers, etc. – and will often create uncomfortable conflict. Understanding your personality type while having a general knowledge of how to identify and deal with other personality types will help to greatly reduce your stress level. More importantly, it will give you an edge towards building healthier relationships.

Your personality type is who you are, the "you" that comes across to other people. Your personality type is always seeking and working to dominate your life. If you do not manage it, it will cause disruption or imbalance within your life. This will become clearer as you continue reading.

CHAPTER 11

The "Me" Personality Type

"Me" types show us how to enjoy life.

Me types are the life of the party and masters at having fun. They set the standard for enjoying life. Me types are the best at socializing and networking. They help us to have a good time at work and at play. They naturally work to change environments toward being more pleasant. Of all the personality types, they are the most prone to risk-taking and adventure. They are also prone to asking the most questions, and a wide variety of questions at that. Hands down, they express themselves verbally the most.

No personality type is more spontaneous than a Me type. They tend to appreciate a less structured lifestyle. What makes a *balanced* Me special is that their primary definition of happiness is based on making others happy. In the end, we all want to learn how to enjoy life, and Me types show us the way. Nothing is as refreshing as talking to or interacting with a pleasant Me when we need customer service. Even when they can't help us, they have a way of making us feel better. This personality type works best as a customer service representative, concierge, or any other position that deals with the general public. I find it interesting that a high percentage of successful comics are Me type personalities. Keeping secrets, especially exciting ones, can be difficult for the Me types. This is mainly because the sheer exuberance they display while having knowledge of the secret is a dead give-away. They prefer that life never has a dull moment.

When Me types do not manage their personality, several imbalances can occur. Imbalanced Me types can be the most selfish of the personality types when they hold their own happiness far above others. They can also be guilty of possessing an "it's all about me and my enjoyment" attitude and not even be aware of it. In a social setting, an imbalanced Me type can be the only one in the room having a good time and wonder why no one else is having fun. When this happens, they can be the most miserable people to be around. Imbalanced Me types can jeopardize the stability of a situation or circumstance due to the short-sightedness of living only for the moment. They often hold others accountable for their unhappiness. Imbalanced Me types often lose sight of and often cannot see the big picture because they judge life by how they are enjoying it at a particular point in time. They live too much in the moment, positively or negatively.

Due to rash decision-making, imbalanced Me's are the first in line to quit, leave or change environments. Imbalanced Me types change relationships, jobs, residences, churches, etc., the most frequently of all the personality types. When it's no longer fun or convenient, an imbalanced Me will seek to escape. Sacrifice and suffering in the short-term for long-term future gains is often difficult for a Me type.

Why manage your Me?
You can't have a balanced life by having fun or even seeking to have fun as a life mission all of the time. Life is serious and avoiding, hiding or even running from important issues will not make them go away and will more than likely make them worse. Accepting responsibility andnot passing the buck or placing blame is a key managing mindset for the Me type who is balanced. Imbalanced Me types always have an excuse. Maintaining a balanced life requires a building mode, where sometimes unpleasant work must be the focus and priority in order to create a brighter and better future. Me types must learn that this fighting stance does not work against enjoyment but rather it helps to ensure long-term enjoyment, pleasure and fun. Living in the moment is great, but there must be boundaries.

Me Type Personalities: Cameron Diaz, Kevin Hart, Will Farrell, Tom Hanks, Chris Rock, Mariah Carey, Jack Nicholson, Robin Williams

Extreme Bright Side (EBS) Me Types:
EBS Me personality types have the ability to turn doom and gloom around. EBS Me types often lift spirits and bring smiles just by entering the room. They can not only disrobe our defense mechanisms, but they have a unique ability to help us relax and let our guard down. Suddenly, the person who doesn't dance is dancing, the person who doesn't laugh is laughing, or the person who never talks is talking. The EBS Me is

unique from other Me types not only for these skills but also for the fact that their definition of having fun is seeking and helping others to have a good time above their own.

Extreme Dark Side (EDS) Me Types:
EDS imbalanced Me types are master manipulators. Taking advantage of people to get their way is the name of the game. Neediness and leeching off of others is a common characteristic. They are master hustlers. An EDS imbalanced Me personality type can overindulge and be prone to seeking the ultimate high or thrill, drifting into addictions or precarious risk-taking situations or lifestyles just for the thrill. Their overindulgence sometimes leads to the loss of everything, including family or their own lives. Everyone within their circle of influence pays the price when the EDS Me is unhappy. All personality types can cheat or cross the flirtation line. However, you can be sure that the EDS Me wrote the book on these negative plights. Living in the moment to the fullest as if it is all there is to life is the calling card of an EDS Me. Additionally, some EDS Me types utilize this calling card differently. Sometimes it causes them to become withdrawn, holding themselves accountable internally for their unhappiness to the point of self-destruction. This is often shocking to loved ones and friends because they are often taken aback due to this being so opposite to the Me personality type.

CHAPTER 12

The "Myself" Personality Type

The *Myself* type shows us how to live safely, with stability.

I have already stated that my core type is Body. My personality type is definitely "Myself." For the Myself personality type, safety, security and stability are paramount above all else in life. Myself types seek out the safest and most secure routes and therefore are the least prone of all the personality types to taking risks. The Myself personality type sets the standard for loyalty and dependability. If a balanced Myself type quits a job for reasons outside of better opportunity, it is safe to assume that things were really bad.

The statement, "throwing caution to the wind," will never be the mindset of the Myself personality type, and caution is the sifter for nearly every action. A Myself type will always take note of where the exits are and will zero in on things that look suspicious or out of sorts. They truly believe that one cannot be too careful. They are naturally very concerned for the safety and protection of others within their circle of influence. Guardians by nature, they are the only personality type that believes some degree of suffering is a natural part of life. Myself personality types may often volunteer to suffer for the greater good of all and sometimes to a fault, suffering unnecessarily.

Being intrusive is sacrilegious for a Myself because they hate being intruded upon themselves. Space and privacy are absolute requirements for a Myself to be happy. Myself types have trust issues and hold being trusted in high esteem. They live a life of high suspicion and remain on high alert for hidden agendas. Drama is a poison to be avoided if at all possible. This personality type seeks to create safe and stable living and working environments and they can become defensive while doing so. Unfortunately, they often have difficulty learning how to enjoy themselves. They tend to be good money, time and risk managers. However, of the three personality types, Myself personalities are the least likely to take risks, frequently envisioning the glass as half-empty versus half-full. They often long for the good ole' days and are often nostalgic. They must avoid being stuck in time due to their resistance to change.

What tends to drive the other personality types crazy about the Myself type is that Myself types not only are comfortable with being alone from time to time, *they actually need alone time.* They are the mysterious ones among the personality types and are the hardest to read or figure out. This causes unwarranted friction at times and some people are just downright uncomfortable being around Myself personality types. In relationships, the other party learns to accept the periodic silence and not take it as being negative or offensive.

Why manage your Myself?
When imbalanced, Myself types can be untrusting and over-protective to a fault. Paranoia, constantly feeling threatened and being overly defensive are all byproducts of imbalanced Myself types. Of all the personality types, they are the most prone to negativity, bitterness, depression and/or isolation. Sometimes these characteristics are almost unnoticeable until it's too late, since most Myself types are introverts. They can be prone to being stuck-in-a-rut from being fearful of change or taking risks even when they clearly are for the better. If it's not broke, imbalanced Myself types often do not want it fixed or improved upon. Myself personality types can push people away by shutting them out, while still blaming others and/or life for their loneliness. Imbalanced Myself types are very insecure. I am reminded of the old joke about the guy who stopped attending football games because every time he saw the team go into a huddle, he thought they were talking about him! Imbalanced Myself types tend to really think the worse when they see people congregate, whisper and look their way.

Learn to relax and let your guard down; socializing is not an attack on you. Do not take rejection as a sign of failure. And, don't take your anger out on the world. Not everyone has a hidden agenda to do you harm. If you do not have friends, do a self-check and don't blame others. The biblical passage in Proverbs 18:24 says, "A man that hath friends must first show himself friendly…" (KJV). Risk-taking is not something that must be avoided but rather just evaluated and weighed against potential benefits.

Myself Personality Types: Prince, Brad Pitt, Angelina Jolie, Tom Cruise, Barak Obama, Mark Zuckerberg, Scarlett Johansen, Adele, Maxwell

Extreme Bright Side (EBS) Myself Types:
EBS Myself types set the bar for trustworthiness, integrity and dependability. No one is better suited to have your back as a friend and/or confidant. They are unique among Myself types in that they truly have your best interest at heart and will sacrifice themselves to protect you. Consistency and predictability are natural characteristics exhibited with pride for the EBS Myself type. They will gravitate naturally to being the moral compass guide for a group as needed. When an EBS Myself says it's bad, then it's really bad. When an EBS Myself says that it's time to panic, then it's time to panic, since they epitomize being cool and calm under pressure. Boring is not necessarily a negative as it is with the other two personality types.

Extreme Dark Side (EDS) Myself Types:
It is no secret that an imbalanced EDS Myself personality type often describes the profiles of serial killers. That is not to say that all EDS Myself types are serial killers, of course. EDS Myself types tend to be almost hermit-like loners, and they are often fearful of rejection by the opposite sex. They tend to be socially awkward, overly defensive and/or have an affinity toward violent imagery and weapons to often mask their heightened fixation and desire for revenge. EDS Myself types will blame others for creating their mindsets or behaviors. Many are paranoid defensive – always assuming people are talking about them or are out to get them. They can become stalkers, obsessive, controlling and even violent regarding that which they feel belongs to them or is owed to them, or that which requires retribution for a perceived wrong done to them.

Since they are hard to figure out and are often labeled as being polite, mannerly and even quiet but kind, their circle of influence tends to be horrified or in shock when they snap and exhibit an extreme outburst.

CHAPTER 13

The "I" Personality Type

Be proud of your accomplishments and control your own destiny.

The "I" personality type is the standard for responsibility, ownership and accountability. I suppose that is why a great many I types achieve some type of leadership status. I would not go as far as to say that they are natural born leaders, but that they are naturally born with the drive to take charge or control in some way, shape or form. Therefore, they push and drive others in a common direction. An I personality type has the ability to sway a person's opinion. For example, oftentimes, in jury trials, a strong I can sway a jury toward a particular point-of-view. They are of the mindset, "Let's get things done." Failure is not an option for an I, and lack of confidence is rarely an area of weakness. They are frequently impatient and have little tolerance for fickle people or those who are okay with just living life without any ambition, drive or direction.

I personality types must be in control over their life and have the loudest voice in their destiny. To I personalities, my present and my future are of equal importance. If I types cannot see the end of a situation, it can impact their happiness in the present. Unlike the Me type, an I type will not be satisfied in the moment no matter how pleasant if it does not tie into a greater plan; to an I, that would be merely settling for less. That is not to say that I types never get caught up in the moment or experience a lack of clarity from time to time, but that would be considered a life lesson that they immediately seek to not allow to happen again. I types usually have a clear vision of where they want to go in life and often expect the same of others.

Taking orders and directions are not strong suits for I types and they will often question authority, which is frequently misinterpreted as being disrespectful. However, questioning authority and having a voice are just natural characteristics of an I personality. They are mission-focused and driven toward accomplishment, achieving goals and being successful above all else. Even when playing games, they tend to forget that it's just a game. It's all about winning in every area of life, at work or at play. I do not want this to be misinterpreted that the other personality types are not as competitive; but the fact is that for an I type, the drive and motivation are different. They possess the killer instinct and drive to win.

For example, Me types tend to want to enjoy the journey along the road to victory as well as the victory. Therefore, they can often struggle with the unpleasant drama along the way. Myself types are constantly weighing the risks and the costs for winning. The question of, "Is it worth the risk?" must be answered correctly for the Myself to be fully motivated to win. Those sentiments are not the case with an I type. If the other personality types say, "Winning isn't everything" or "It's not just did you lose but how did you lose?" I types see it as "Winning is everything and sometimes it is the only thing!"

I types have a propensity to recommend or tell you what you should or shouldn't do. They will definitely inform you of their accomplishments and abilities or how they can make things happen for the better.

Why manage your I?
When an I type is imbalanced, they can be overly competitive or possess a skewed view that everything or everyone is a challenge! They forget that it's not always about being in control or in charge. Imbalanced I types feel completely lost or that they are a failure if they don't feel in control or in charge. They can be prone to "authoritative attitudes" and are oftentimes control freaks. Imbalanced I personality types are masters of "my way or the highway" or "win at all cost" behaviors, and they develop their own rules and break the established ones along the way. Many times, they are instigators of conflict, where they often gain a sense of self-worth from winning situations of conflict that they created or imagined themselves. This worsens as their self-confidence falters. They can be very dismissive of others' thoughts and ideas.

Imbalanced I personality types frequently look down on people and can be too judgmental or critical. Oftentimes, they perceive themselves as being in charge when, in fact, they literally have lost the control and respect of the group, situation or circumstance. They can be caught up in the feeling of control rather than the reality of actually being in control. An example would be a football coach who is still demanding and yelling, but his team has totally tuned him out. At some point during the constant barrage of putdowns and reminders of shortcomings and belittling, the team loses all respect for the overbearingcoach. The coach feels in control but has actually lost control.

I Personality Types: Donald Trump, Muhammed Ali, Nancy Grace, John Wayne, Suze Orman, Kobe Bryant, Wendy Williams, Charles Barkley, James Brown

Extreme Bright Side (EBS) I Types:
They make up a large percentage of the demographic of successful entrepreneurs, coaches and business owners. Stories of someone taking charge in dire situations are often examples of EBS I types, including in times of tragedy such as strategically leading people to counter-attack the assailant or turning around the business enterprise that was perceived to be unsalvageable. EBS I types thrive on the challenge of the impossible and turning it around with success that positively impacts large groups of people.

Extreme Dark Side (EDS) I Types:
Imbalanced EDS I types are the epitome of control freaks and bullies. Threatening intimidation is their modus operandi. They tend to believe that everyone and anyone can be replaced, including loved ones. The attitude that "I don't need anyone else because no one is as good as me" or "I'm not going out like that" is representative of the self-centeredness of the EDS I type. Even when they have to face the reality of losing, they have to control how they lose. Oftentimes, they feel humiliated and respond in violent ways. Although the personality type of the EDS Myself is more prominent in serial killers, vulgar crimes of passion or revenge are more prominent with the Extreme Dark Side I types. Think: "If I can't have you, then no one can" or "I own you." Challenging the human limits of pain, sexual acts, endurance, etc., in a demented manner are also found to be more prevalent within this group as they pursue conquering all.

Jury selection

I think utilizing this personality type breakdown would be very helpful when choosing a jury. The power of personality is often underestimated. It is even more important than the beliefs and values of the jury pool. Why? Because your personality type gives insight into your belief system, which is more important because we cannot possibly ask all of the questions that will truly categorize beliefs adequately in the limited time available for jury pool evaluation and selection.

What if the jury pool has more than a few Myself types? If the trial has a strong element of safety or security issues, wouldn't the Myself have strong opinions on such matters? If the jury is weighted with Me types, then a trial that belittles the defendant for participating in some sort of risqué fun activity would be viewed perhaps as picking on the defendant. As far as strong I types are concerned, well, I do not have the numbers but I am sure that a large number of hung juries were caused by a defiant to the end I type. My point is that an equal distribution of the three personality types should be pursued when selecting a jury pool. Even if that goal is not met, it would still be an improvement over the current process.

Dining out

The next time you eat out, try to figure out the personality of your server. This common interaction provides good practice ground for identifying personality types. Typically the Me type will be more talkative and prone to discuss more than what is on the menu. They love the question, "Well, what do you like or recommend?" Sidebar conversations will often enhance their service. The Myself will speak the least and will never recommend a menu item without being asked first. They may even answer the question awkwardly with something like, "Well, what do you like?" They tend to stick to the service protocol and grow increasingly uncomfortable the more that the interaction goes out of the norm. The I types will recommend a dish or make a suggestion even when you did not ask or desire one. I types will also answer your questions with strong absolutes when they know that something can or cannot be done.

CHAPTER 14

How to Manage Your Personality Type

At this point, it is important to state once again that there are three facets that make up everyone's personality. It is just that one facet tends to outweigh the other two, which I define as being your personality type. If I may use the vehicle comparison again, the difference between your core type and your personality type is that your core type is the kind of vehicle you are, and your personality type is the style of driver you are. In other words, if you drive an SUV at high speeds around sharp turns, you are at risk of rolling over. By the same token, if you consistently drive a sports car over rough terrain, you risk damaging your vehicle.

Therefore, by managing your personality, you become a better driver of your life so to speak. This entails disciplining yourself to not give in to the first impulse reaction of your personality type. You must learn how to tap into the other two facets and use them. Remember, you do not have to help your personality type! It is always seeking to control and direct all that you do. Your personality type sets the rules of engagement for how you approach your day. It needs no assistance and it is always on auto-pilot, raring to go. Your personality type just oozes out of you and is always willing and able to show itself. It wants to rule.

However, your personality type must be resisted, controlled and disciplined. Or else, it will be unhealthy and imbalanced when making decisions. Me personality types cannot have fun all of the time. There are real-life situations that are just unpleasant and have to be addressed. Procrastination, avoidance and constant shifting are all signs of an imbalanced Me type. Inconsistency and instability, including experiencing frequent highs and lows, are frequent symptoms of imbalanced Me types. They cannot allow the Me part of them to take over and drive them toward seeking fun and enjoyment at all cost (think: reckless driving).

A Myself personality type cannot be so cautious and adverse to risk-taking that they never progress or even, more importantly, learn to enjoy life. Yes, life is dangerous, but no one can avoid and/or eliminate all danger. If a Myself type is not careful, they will be so consumed with safety and caution that they never progress or experience all that life has to offer. Imbalanced Myself types build cocoons of isolation, often pushing others away inadvertently. Expressions of "leave me alone" and not answering doors or phones for long periods of time are signs of an imbalanced Myself type. They are the drivers who navigate through life in fear or nervousness, clenching their steering wheels while driving, wondering why everyone drives so fast, and asking why others do not stay in their own lanes. It is okay to be cautious, but please remember to allow for spontaneity in your life. Resist being defensive or becoming offended.

Not to be forgotten, the I personality type must realize that they will always have an opinion or question regarding power or authority, but must learn to resist the temptation to always speak out or react. Most of the time, taking charge is rarely needed and often not wise. There are other ways to get answers and find success. "Going with the flow" is not a crime, and you will still reach your destination successfully. You may even gain a few more friends along the way. Please realize that others may perceive you to be overbearing and controlling even when it is not your intention. Counteract this by being sensitive to what is being said instead of instinctively jumping to a conclusion. Remember, being in charge and feeling in charge are not the same thing. Additionally, having the loudest or strongest voice does not automatically equate to being the most respected voice.

In short, seek out and strategize ways to engage and display your two secondary personality facets. This is critical in attaining and maintaining a balanced life. If I had to put percentages on the demographic breakdown of personality types, I would say that 30 percent are Me, 40 percent are Myself, and roughly 20 percent of the global populace are in the I category. The remaining 10 percent consist of what I call "multi-personalities."

CHAPTER 15

Multi-Personalities

Before I get into multi-personalities, let me say that although your core type does not and cannot change, I do believe that your personality type can change. Some personalities even change between childhood and adulthood. In other circumstances, maturation entities or experiences can change a personality, as in going to boarding school or serving in the military, for instance. Traumatic experiences can change your personality type as well.

I have noticed something regarding this over the years. In most cases, the person merely learns how to tap into and use another facet of their personality more, and their dominant personality type does not really change. For instance, the person who needed to learn how to speak up and be counted more learns how to tap into and utilize their I personality facet. They do not really become an I type.

Cases where I have observed true personality type changes were of people who were another type but became a Myself type. The "Exhibit A" example that I have used throughout the years is the awesomely talented Will Smith. When I first started this journey of developing the principles for this book almost twenty years ago, Will was in my opinion the ultimate Me personality type. Today he does not exhibit quite the same exuberant, fun-loving, always laughing, life is a party personality. Today he is more the prime example of a Myself personality type as a result of his life and personal experiences. He is much more guarded now, and even his movie roles tend to reflect that to some degree.

Some people have what I call multi-personalities (not to be confused with the medical condition - Multiple Personality Disorder), meaning they can fluctuate within two or more of the personality types as if each one were the dominant personality. Many of us have witnessed this and can recall individuals within our minds. The majority of these individuals do not have a medical condition. My purpose is not to address medical Multiple Personality Disorder issues.

Qualified medical professionals should be consulted in those cases. I believe that multi-personalities are also reflected in the biblical term, "variance." Multi-personalities can drift between two or more of the personality facets as result of fantasy, core damage, or as a reactionary defense mechanism against pain, loss or embarrassment.

People with multi-personalities learn to function within society and even to advance their careers, but their circle of relationships will usually remain small due to the inability to consistently allow their dominant personality type to shine through. In other words, there tends to always be a storm brewing inside that will come out when the group atmospheric conditions are right. Extreme personality type swings have the same impact as extreme mood swings: they both push people away. Counseling can be an effective aid towards achieving life balance in such cases.

PART FOUR

Core & Personality Type Combinations, The Launch and Lift-Off

CHAPTER 16

Core & Personality Type Combinations

In pop culture, there is a gamut of personalities we can relate to when exploring and identifying core types and personality types. Before we get to that, let's quickly analyze the core and personality type combinations (the what and who you are).

The Core / Personality Type Combinations

Spirit/Me
Usually high energy, inquisitive, fun-loving and providers of sunshine on a dreary day. But do not let the happy-go-lucky appearance fool you. When upset, this core/personality type combination can show high intensity of anger when upset. They are the most talkative of all the core/personality type combinations.

Spirit/I
Usually dominating, always assertive and sometimes aggressive. Winning is everything; this core/personality type does not take challenges or mistreatment lightly and does not back down from a fight. They are the most prone to speak up and challenge. The ability to rally or move a group is strong due to their need to be seen and heard. This group represents the most forceful core/personality type combination.

Spirit/Myself
Very guarded and reserved due to the fact that they can be hurt or offended more easily than the other core/personality types. They are naturally thin-skinned and it has to thicken over time. They take pride in avoiding being offensive, but they are often defensive. Spirit/Myself types tend to be very cautious and pessimistic. They need very few friends but have a high desire to be well liked and accepted. Although they enjoy alone time, they have a great fear of being in a state of loneliness. This core/personality type is often difficult to identify due the fact that the great majority of Spirits are extroverts, only the Spirit/Myself is an introvert. They are unique introverts in that, like a faucet, once the comfort valve is opened, they can be as chatty as the other Spirit personality types, like lightening in a bottle.

Mind/Me
Energetic but calculating drivers of enjoyment and having fun. Winning does not consume them, but they are rather focused on how the game is played or on enjoying the journey to the goal. They are prone to seeking to find the way that people can accomplish the goal together. They should be careful not to be so wrapped up in their own version of reality that they ignore the warning signs from the outside. Do not fall into the trap of being a legend in your own mind.

Mind/I
Accomplishment focused, goal oriented and prone to teach others. Calculating in their relationships. Although they hold friendship in high esteem, they require only a few close friendships. They are self-motivated and driven, but appreciate positive response from others.

Mind/Myself
Strong-willed and guarded. They will not seek to necessarily get involved but will when asked. They will exhibit an openness and enthusiasm rarely seen when involved with causes or situations they are passionate about.

Body/Me
Enthusiastic and willing to help. Hobbies and interests that require physical effort and work motivate them the most.

Body/I
Perhaps the rarest of the core/personality types. They are intense in attaining short-term goals and pursuits. They are prone to do it or attempt to do it all themselves when important physical activity must get done. This core/personality combination must be cognizant not to burn their core out, in other words their bodies.

Body/Myself
Slowly but surely is the way with this type. Life is the tortoise versus the hare story. They believe in building life one brick at a time. Energetic regarding passions and interests, they approach everything else with

cautious optimism. Not wasting physical energy and reserving strength for matters of importance is a priority for this core/personality type.

Hybrid Core
Having a dual core with one side always being Spirit. Utilize the appropriate definitions for your Hybrid cores and personality types.

Multi-personality
Having your core side with a combination of two or more personality facets exhibited almost simultaneously on a regular basis.

Throughout the book, I have listed famous people who represent the various core and personality types. Since we all are a dual combination of core type and personality type (recall our vehicle type and kind of driver example) let us take a look at some pop culture examples to help us better grasp the concepts.

Pop Culture Examples
"American Idol"

American Idol was a recent long running reality television show where contestants competed in an amateur singing contest weekly with the end goal of being the last person standing thus becoming the "American Idol." A recording contract and other prizes were part of the winnings. Let us take a look at some of the judges.

The initial judges were Simon Cowell, Paula Abdul and Randy Jackson. First up is Simon, his blunt criticism was often too much for both con-testants and the audience to bear. If he felt that the contestant had little or no talent, he was quick to cut to the chase and let the contestant know what he thought. If the contestant had talent he would let them know that succinctly as well. To Simon, the delivery of the message was not nearly as important as the message itself. He deemed the emotional aspect of the interaction as being insignificant. Simon was also quick to refer to his credentials and experience to emphasize his point or to put someone in their place.

He is a Mind/I.

Paula Abdul definitely felt for the contestants. The sincerity and passion expressed by the contestants were worthy of recognition in her evaluation of them. She exhibited a high level of emotional energy all wrapped up in a bubbly happy go lucky demeanor. *She is a Spirit/Me.*

Randy Jackson was often the man in the middle of the disagreeing Simon and Paula. He seemed to bring calmness and stability to the team when things occasionally turned rocky. Randy would talk through the specifics in a logical and non-threatening manner. *He is a Mind/Myself.*

Later judges on the show included Jennifer Lopez and Mariah Carey among others. Jennifer showed emotion but more than that she articulated her thoughts more than her feelings. Her personality seems to be guarded as if expressive only by her permission. *She is a Mind/Myself.*

It would not be prudent to by-pass the host of the show, Ryan Seacrest. His out-going and fun loving personality cemented the engagement of the contestants, judges and viewers. That was not an easy task at all. He did it in a thoughtful way with the tactful goal of bringing smiles and laughter, while avoiding other emotions. *He is a Mind/Me.*

"Sex and the City"

Now let us consider the former hit HBO original series, "Sex and the City," to further evaluate core and personality types. The show's premise follows a sex columnist and her three friends as they navigate through New York's dating scene.

Let's do a quick study of the four main characters. Consider Carrie Bradshaw, the sex columnist. A heavy thinker often consumed with reflecting. Carrie usually finds herself in inner conflict due to a strong desire to have a good time, which overrides logic. Happiness is her motivation for life even when it doesn't make logical sense. After landing her dream guy, Carrie does not realize the amount of work required to maintain a happy relationship. *She is a Spirit/Me.*

Take a look at Samantha. My first instinct was to identify her as a Body core type because she is consumed with discussing physical interaction. However, sexiness is first and foremost in her mind, above any other emotional and physical drive. She is a Me because her desire to have a good time is always a high priority, throwing both caution and control to the wind. Yes, she wants control but first and foremost is her enjoyment and fantasy. That pursuit is not typical for an I personality type. If she used intimacy as a means to gain power and control, that would reflect an I type, but she does not. *She is a Mind/Me.*

Now, examine Charlotte. She has a very intense, emotional center, which shows whether she is excited, angry or sad. Charlotte's personality is transparent, being revealed constantly. She is the cautious, protective and on-guard defender who is always seeking the safest, most stable route. This hypersensitive character respects any and all walks of life. *She is a Spirit/Myself.*

Our final character study here is Miranda. Iron-willed and strong–minded, Miranda is always rationalizing and passing judgment. She tries to understand and make mental sense of everything via reasoning. Miranda is determined, focused and demands control of her own life's direction and destiny. She is driven to accomplishment, emphasizing self-sustainment and needing no one. Oftentimes, Miranda finds herself feeling alone due to her controlling personality. She is a great example of how managing your personality brings balance to interpersonal relationships. Her eventual relationship blossoms as she taps into other facets of her personality. She learns that it is only settling for less when you find yourself unhappy after managing your personality. Miranda does not settle; she learns how to guard and manage. *She is a strong Mind/I.*

The Peanuts Gang

The *Peanuts* characters, created by Charles M. Schulz, have placed an indelible imprint on America's heart. Much like a rainbow exudes hues of many colors, these beloved animated characters possess a vast array of personalities.

Charlie Brown is a complex character, which may be one reason why he is adored around the world. Identifying Charlie's core type was more challenging than I first anticipated. I believe he is a Mind in that he really pushes to think logically. On the other hand, his emotional decision-making often makes no sense when the evidence clearly shows that the end results will not be positive. Even though he knows that Lucy will move the ball before he kicks it, he still attempts to "go for it" if the feeling is right. Sometimes, he falls right into Lucy's trap, while other times, it takes a little bit of coaxing. Nevertheless, he always ends up on his back while Lucy yells, "You're a blockhead, Charlie Brown!" Charlie enjoys being alone, pondering life's dilemma. His personality type is clearly a Myself. I would say that Charlie is a *Hybrid (Mind/Spirit)/Myself*.

Let's consider Charlie Brown's loveable Beagle, Snoopy. A friend indeed, Snoopy is constantly striving to help others through their difficult situations. From helping Charlie search for Christmas trees, to assisting Woodstock in building new nests, Snoopy is a logical thinker and a reasoning strategist. At the same time, Snoopy enjoys having a good time. Known as "Joe Cool" and the World War I "Flying Ace," Snoopy possesses an extremely vivid imagination. *He is a Mind/Me.*

Now, take a look at Snoopy's best friend, Woodstock. This is one animal who definitely wears his feelings on his sleeve. If he is sad, he cries, and whenever he is upset, he throws a temper tantrum, and when he is excited, his exuberance causes him to fall because he laughs so hard. Observing the interaction between Woodstock and Snoopy is very similar to watching typical "best friends" balance each other. Full of fire and energy, Woodstock sometimes acts erratic due to his nervous spirit. Outside of Snoopy, he prefers being alone. *He is a Spirit/Myself.*

Let us examine Charlie Brown's best friend, Linus van Pelt. At first glance, Linus is the logical-thinking, reasoning one, often deep into his own thoughts. Usually, Linus shows little to no emotion. But, once you take away his security blanket, Linus hyperventilates and nearly loses his mind. Although a good friend and confidant to Charlie Brown, Linus is equally fine with being alone. *He is a Mind/Myself.*

Hands down, Lucy van Pelt has the strongest personality of the entire Peanuts Gang. With Lucy, we witness the dominant personality of an I personality type in full bloom. Lucy is the loudest and most confronta-tional. She is a fighting Spirit, who constantly dictates orders to the group at-large. Charlie Brown and Linus both feel the brunt whenever mistakes are made. Lucy's entrepreneurial spirit often leads her to open outdoor lemonade and "advice" (psychiatric) stands. Although known for fre-quently playing "mind games" with her friends, Lucy is not a Mind but rather a hurricane Spirit. She is the ultimate I personality type. Moreover, her authoritative attitude is fueled by her emotional fire. Lucy is a *Spirit/I.*

Let's take a look at Patricia "Peppermint Patty" Reichardt. *Peanuts* creator and animator Charles M. Schulz described this character as the one who "goes through life wearing blinders." Patty is what we call an "emotional being," who feels and dreams without seeing the obvious. For example, she has had a longstanding crush on Charlie Brown. However, he has given her every indication that his feelings are not mutual, and he often wonders if Patty has one or two screws loose! Despite the obvious, Patty also insists that Snoopy is a "weird-looking kid." She's not cognizant that Snoopy is actually a dog. Patty is the best athlete, who also enjoys social interaction and playing games, but she does not seek to be in charge. As the bravest of the *Peanuts* characters, she has no problem standing up to Lucy. In fact, she effectively ignores her as if they both know that Lucy is no match. If Ms. Patty chose to get angry, everyone in the room could be in trouble. Unique indeed, she is a *Spirit/Me*.

Lastly, let us examine Schroeder, the musical prodigy. He is always focused on his piano and playing classical music. Whenever Charlie Brown needs a pep talk, Schroeder gives him motivational speeches on the baseball mound. No matter how many sweet nothings Lucy whispers in Schroeder's ear, he has no response and is often perturbed about her leaning on his piano. *He is a Mind/Myself.*

Here are a few more examples of pop culture figures and their respective core and personality types:

PERSONALITY TYPE	CORE TYPE Body	CORE TYPE Mind	CORE TYPE Spirit
Me	*	Ellen DeGeneres LeBron James Tom Hanks Beyoncé Jack Nicholson	Cameron Diaz Mariah Carey Robin Williams Kevin Hart Magic Johnson Cam Newton
Myself	Derrick Rose* Marshawn Lynch*	Kim Kardashian Barack Obama Dustin Hoffman Tom Cruise Anthony Hopkins Angelina Jolie Mark Zuckerberg Aaron Rogers Tom Brady Tiger Woods Ted Cruz	Kanye West Sarah Palin Nicki Minaj Mike Tyson
I	*	Kobe Bryant Simon Cowell Charles Barkley Madonna Steve Jobs Suze Orman	Donald Trump Muhammed Ali Nancy Grace Stephen A. Smith Russell Westbrook James Brown

*As I have stated throughout this book, it is difficult to identify the Body core type without knowing them personally.

A Word on Relationships

Inevitably, I am always asked about relationships. People always want to figure out which core/personality type is best suited for them. I usually respond with, "Come on, do you really think the answer to the complex relationship success equation is that simple?" There are no magical or scientific guarantees for relationships. The principles outlined within this book will not provide the yellow brick road to your ideal mate.

These principles provide you with insight to better understand yourself, your partner and those around you. If nothing else, you now understand that you cannot change your significant other. I do believe, however, that if you reflect back on your past that may be littered with failed relationships, you will probably see a pattern with core and/or personality types in those failures. Although these principles will not tell you who you should be with, they can possibly tell you the core and/or personality type that is the most challenging for you. However, I wouldn't recommend pre-judging if you have not experienced a certain core and personality type. I could not have predicted that I would be happily married to an I personality type. In fact, she is a very balanced Mind/I.

For a balanced relationship, both parties should help each other guard and manage. You can help guard your significant other's core type, even as they work to guard it themselves.

For example, since I am a Body core type, my wife observes when I am over-extending myself and will at times recommend that I get some rest. Fatigue with me causes grumpiness. By the same token, if she is really hungry, she can barely think straight. Perhaps the best thing that we do regarding each other's core type is that we are able to see past temper flare ups, sarcastic remarks and outbursts when we notice that each other's core is being attacked or is stressed. We do not overreact and respond negatively in these cases. It can be as simple as a bad day on the job or dealing with a serious family issue. When your partner's core is stressed or under attack, they are not themselves, so it would be unfair to overreact to tension during those times. Couples need to work together to find ways to guard, nurture and care for each other's core. When pursued with love, it sets the foundation and structure for a far stronger and greater lasting relationship.

Regarding the personality type side, you cannot manage your partner's personality type for them. However, you can encourage them to manage for themselves and you can accept them for who they are and respectfully nurture it. For example, I commonly hear from couples that "he or she is childish, plays around too much and never takes me seriously." The other party in turn will respond with something like, "They need to lighten up. It is the classic Me vs. Myself type clash. The Myself must accept that a Me will never be as serious about life and its situations. It's just not in their DNA wiring. You will become frustrated and waste a lot of time.

What you can do is make sure that you participate in what makes the Me in the relationship happy from an enjoyment and fun standpoint. I warn couples that it is not wise when a Me in a relationship can name their top three regular fun activities and their significant other never wants to participate in any of them. By the same token, the Me in this case must realize that, although a Myself may have to manage taking life and its circumstances too seriously, they still will always have priorities set in order for them to feel safe, secure and stable within the relationship. The Me should find ways to honor those priorities. Relationships with an I personality type will find that success for them will challenge the classic definitions and paradigms expected of relationships. Individuality will certainly be seen more in such relationships.

These are just small examples of how two individuals can work together to manage their own personality while nurturing their partner's, thereby enjoying one another's company more.

The Achilles' heel for personality types in one word:
- Me - Selfishness
- Myself - Offense (being offended or defensive)
- I - Pride (arrogance)

When you are dealing with personality types in relationship conflict:
- ❖ The main challenge with Me types will be for you to convince them
- ❖ The main challenge with Myself types will be for you to understand them
- ❖ The main challenge with I types will be for you to know how to handle or take them

If relationship issues are not rectified, then:
- ❖ The Me type is inclined to wander or grow apart from the relationship
- ❖ The Myself type is inclined to shut down and fall away from the relationship
- ❖ The I type is inclined to tear or break down the relationship

Misidentification

I am often asked if I have ever misidentified someone. My answer is yes and quite often, at that. These days, I am approached by people who ask me all the time to help them identify both their and others' core and personality types and, more often than not, I have limited information. Some people think that after a brief encounter or two, they really have you figured out and they think they know you. They often expect you to do the same. As I have tried to emphasize throughout this book, we far too often flash with prideful glee our supposed ability to size people up and figure them out completely. Most of the time, however, we are simply rushing to judgment with incomplete information.

In the early days as I developed these principles, of course plenty of mistakes were made even within my own family. Additionally, multi-personality issues can be tricky to sort through, and well-balanced people can be so even keeled that it can be difficult to identify their core in a short amount of time. For instance, Myself personality types can often mask their core. Sometimes, if they are significantly introverted and withdrawn, Myself personality types can suppress emotions if they are a Spirit core, to the point that they rarely show how they feel in normal day-to-day activity.

This is neither a science nor a medical book and it is not intended to be. The pop culture names and examples mentioned within for identifying certain core and personality types, are opinions, and that means of course that they are open to being differing types.

CHAPTER 17

The Launch and Lift-Off

Important points to remember as you launch forward.

The goal of this book is to be a launching pad. It is then not fitting to call the last chapter the conclusion or wrap-up. Some of the information may be difficult to digest. Reflection, thought and even meditation may be required as you grapple and reconcile with your own life as well as the lives of those within your circle of influence. It is befitting, then, that I close with a concise review and some parting words.

You must guard your core and manage your personality type in order to attain to and maintain a balanced life (reaching goals and building strong interpersonal relationships). Business/Career goals and personal relationship success are related, but they are not the same. You may have heard the old adage, "a public success, but a private failure." That is a powerful statement that distinguishes the differences but also emphasizes the important connection between "core type" and "personality type." In the end, we all want both *public* and *private* success for a well-balanced life. So, take your time to openly and honestly identify, learn and then engage strategies on how to guard your core and manage your personality.

Points to remember regarding Core Types
Your core is what you are, the all-encompassing factor for how you live and manage your daily life. In review, there are three core facets: Mind, Spirit and Body. We all have them but for most of us, one of the three is clearly the overriding factor for our life balance. When your core suffers, your whole balance of life is off kilter. So, you must learn to guard and nurture your core.

The core breakdown for the global population is as follows:
- ❖ Spirits = 50%
- ❖ Minds = 30%
- ❖ Bodies = 15%
- ❖ Hybrids = 5%

Pitfalls to avoid when identifying your own or someone else's core type include:

- ❖ If you are a Spirit, you may be tempted to prove yourself as being a Mind. Remember that a Spirit's tendency to reflect and ponder is not the definition of a Mind. A Spirit should be open and honest with the fact that their inner wellbeing and how they feel within their emotions and feelings is what drives them the most. Also recall that Spirit cores operate within one of two spectrums: fight – prone to be assertive by speaking out or taking actions; or flight – prone to withdrawal and going into a quiet, sad or depressed shell.

- ❖ Avoid the rush to judgment that you are a Hybrid. Hybrids are less than 5 percent of the population.

- ❖ The Hybrid will always include a Spirit core as part of their dual combination.

- ❖ When trying to identify someone else's core, remember that Body types are the most difficult to ascertain due to the fact that we all show the same physical symptoms and expressions when our bodies are under attack. For the Body, the difference is the magnitude of the impact and how it affects one's ability to accomplish things of importance. Identifying others as a Body usu- ally requires knowing the person very well or to be in a position to observe them on a regular basis, such as working side by side with a co-worker. Being a Body has nothing to do with physical fitness, nor does it have anything to do with being a lazy person.

- ❖ Being a Mind has nothing to do with measuring intelligence. Intelligence is the ability to acquire and apply knowledge and skills. All cores can certainly do that. No one core has an advantage in that area. Being a Mind core type simply means that you are instinctively prone to react mentally the most frequent and longest before you feel the emotional rise or physical response or reaction. Minds first and foremost apply logical, systematic reasoning usually without consideration of feelings first. Personal perspectives on the boundaries of right, wrong, good and bad are firmly entrenched within a Mind's thinking. Sometimes, they assume they already know the feelings of others. Minds should be careful not to exhibit a pattern of dismissing the feelings of others, or being too quick to pass judgment due to impatience.

Points to remember regarding Personality Types

All of us exhibit all three personality facets. However, one will typically stand out above the other two and be the dominant one. If your core is your vehicle type, then your personality is the type of driver you are. How you relate to others and how you feel about yourself is driven by your personality type.

The personality type breakdown of the populace is as follows:
- ❖ Me = 30%
- ❖ Myself = 40%
- ❖ I = 20%
- ❖ Multi-personality = 10%

Pitfalls to avoid regarding your personality type include:
- **Me** – Balanced Me types light up the room. Their main definition of having fun is helping others have a good time. Be careful that you are not selfishly the only one in the room enjoying yourself. Selfishness is the Achilles' heel of an imbalanced Me.

- **Myself** – A balanced Myself prioritizes security and stability for others as well as themselves. However, make sure that doing so does not get to the point of being overbearing or paranoid. Life is not about pursuing the elimination of any and all risk-taking and spontaneity – both of which are important for life progression, fulfillment and relationship balance. Avoid being defensive and shutting down. These responses are oftentimes caused by overreacting, which is a common pitfall of an imbalanced Myself.

- **I** – Be sure that your assertiveness, leadership and confidence are also building up the confidence of others. Otherwise, your road to success may be littered with broken hearts and spirits of others, with those you love being hurt the most. Take caution that you do not become too controlling, domineering and overbearing, which can even be done by accident. Be more open to the ideas and opinions of others.

You May Commence Lift-Off

I sincerely hope you have enjoyed this explorative journey. The book's ending is not meant to be a conclusion but rather a launching pad for your lift-off into your own journey of self-discovery and personal development. My hope also is for you to be enthusiastically engaged as you reach for a better understanding of those within your circle of influence and those in the world around you.

Utilize the tools given to build stronger relationships with family, friends, co-workers and beyond. Some self-help and spiritual books are written by Minds for Minds, assuming that we can all apply the same mental strategies for self-improvement. However, that is not the case since the average reader will be a Spirit core type. Therefore, this book tries to speak both to the Mind and Spirit. For my readers with spouses or significant others, I smile to myself as I reflect on the numerous "ah ha" moments in counseling couples and the light came on – "So that's why they act that way."

For managers, could it be that a certain employee is really not being disrespectful or challenging your leadership? Could they merely be an I personality type? What about that employee you can't seem to motivate?

When was the last time you did something fun for your team? The problem could be that simple if you have a lot of Me personality types. Or do you have a lot of Spirit core types on your team? If so, there is no motivation better for Spirits than showing expressions of appreciation. Perhaps a certain reader now can begin to understand and relate to their boss better. Do not be intimidated by their I personality; start stroking that ego of theirs a little bit. It may provide the pressure relief valve that helps you get through your day better.

Are you a parent who is burnt out from trying to control your fiery little Spirit core type? Remember to seek and develop containment strategies rather than control. Spirits respond to voluntary containment and will always resist control.

Lastly, may you never rush to judge a person again without first evaluating their core and personality types

Five. Four. Three. Two. One. Lift-off!

Acknowledgments

This book is a result of divine inspiration and a consolidation of unique life experiences. I would like to thank my wife, Tatiana, God's gift to me, who provided the main motivation and inspiration for my writing this book. She would always say, "The world needs to hear this."

Thank you to Pastor Harold Hoffman of Sterling Heights, Michigan, for teaching me how to operate with the spirit of excellence; and Pastor Stephen Hamilton of San Fernando, California, for providing the platform and canvas for me to fine tune, create and expand.

Next, I offer sincere gratitude and thanks to all of the teams I have led and developed during my managerial years in corporate America. There were indeed many, but special thanks to the Eaton Aerospace, Hamilton Sundstrand, B/E Aerospace and Meggitt Quality Assurance teams. Your cooperation, trust and respect while garnering our victories in moving and improving the quality system forward are appreciated and will never be forgotten. You also provided the practice field for me to develop the concepts and principles within this book. I would like to thank my many work managers, leaders and customers.

Also thank you to my good friends, Reggie, Lance and Carlos, for being a real support and my comrades over the years. You three know my story indeed, because in many instances you jumped into the trenches with me. Thank you for not just standing by and watching but jumping in to assist during my many biblical story of Job like experiences.

Thank you to my children and family near and far, especially those of you who spoke a word of encouragement regarding this book along the way. Sincere thanks to my publishing team led by Willa Robinson of Knowledge Power Books for their work and support and to my uncle Ray and cousin Tami for their invaluable proof edit input.

In loving memory of my daughter, Camille, who would have been twenty-five years old at the time of book release.

Moreover, I want to express indescribable gratitude in loving memory of my mother, Juanita Payne, and the late Bishop Norman L. Wagner. They were the two most influential and admired people in my life.

Finally, above all else, thanks be to God from whom all blessings flow. He has brought the dream to pass.

About the Author

Jay Payne worked over thirty years in several progressive Quality Assurance capacities within various manufacturing industries, including food, automotive, commercial, industrial and aerospace. He is a graduate of Purdue University and he spent his final manufacturing years as a Director of Quality. Jay has also served in various capacities of the clergy for over 25 years. He was once a full-time single parent of three children who are now adults, one of whom is deceased. Conducting life coaching, counseling and providing spiritual insight are his passions. Improving the Quality Assurance of people's lives is his aim. Because of his life's story, Jay has been compared by several who are familiar with his life, to the biblical story of Job. He resides in the South Bay area of Southern California with his beautiful wife, Tatiana. Correspondence should be sent to:

T & J Oneness
6285 E. Spring St. #331N Long Beach, CA 90808
Facebook: tandjoneness
Email: tandjoneness@cox.net

Bibliography

"Peanuts." Wikipedia: The Free Encyclopedia. Wikimedia Foundation, Inc. 8th October, 2015 Web.8 Oct.2015.https://en.wikipedia.org/wiki/Peanuts

Holy Bible: King James Version

www.ingramcontent.com/pod-product-compliance
Lightning Source LLC
Chambersburg PA
CBHW070632300426
44113CB00010B/1744